STORYBOOKS FOR *Caring* PARENTS

Angry, But Not Too Angry (to talk)

Dave Jackson

Illustrated by Susan Lexa

Chariot Books
DAVID C. COOK PUBLISHING CO.

To Jamie

Chariot Books is an imprint of David C. Cook Publishing Co.
David C. Cook Publishing Co., Elgin, Illinois 60120
David C. Cook Publishing Co., Weston, Ontario

ANGRY, BUT NOT TOO ANGRY
© 1985 by Dave Jackson for the text and Susan Lexa for the illustrations.
All rights reserved. Except for brief excerpts for review purposes, no part of this book may be reproduced or used in any form without written permission from the publisher.
Cover photo by Bakstad Photographics

First printing, 1985
Printed in the United States of America
89 88 87 86 85   5 4 3 2 1

Library of Congress Cataloging in Publication Data

Jackson, Dave.
  Angry, but not too angry (to talk).

  (Storybooks for caring parents)
  Summary: Stories with accompanying Scripture quotations and discussion questions suggest ways to deal with anger over unfair punishment, conflict with a bully, and damage done by a young sibling.
    1. Anger—Religious aspects—Christianity—Juvenile literature. 2. Christian life—1960—Juvenile literature. [1. Anger. 2. Behavior. 3. Christian life.]
I. Lexa, Susan, ill. II. Title. III. Series.
BV4627.A5J33 1985   241'.3   84-27455
ISBN 0-89191-960-0

Scripture references identified (NIV) are from the New International Version.

Contents

For Parents

This Storybook for Caring Parents is written to help your children know how to cope with anger. The approach found here avoids the extremes of either repressing anger or venting it. Instead, these stories will help your children identify their angry feelings and communicate them in appropriate ways—ways that lead toward resolution and reconciliation.

The introductory section offers insights and suggestions for you, the parent. The three stories that follow are for you to read aloud to your children. At the end of each, you'll find thought questions and ideas to discuss. Use them; talk about the stories with your children. Let "angry, but not too angry to talk" become a slogan they will remember and use.

Late Again

In this story, Jamie thinks that his mother is punishing him unfairly by not letting him go to his friend's house just because he was ten minutes late getting home from school. At first he is so angry he yells and accuses, but after some time alone to cool down he can speak respectfully and does. His explanation for his lateness actually proves to be an acceptable one, and he is allowed to go play.

Controlling anger enough to speak respectfully and tell how one feels doesn't mean repression. It is, rather, the way to get the most positive results in correcting the situation. Quiet time alone is often one of the best ways for a person to regain control of his or her emotions.

In the story, the mother hastily assumes that Jamie is late for no good reason. But her willingness to ask for forgiveness is an important example to Jamie.

Not every attempt to talk out a problem leads to "getting to go play." Sometimes disappointment remains. But if there is any hope at all of true resolution, it will come only through communication—talking.

Windy Britches

Each day on his way home from school, Jamie is jumped on by a gang of three boys. When his father finds out, he sits down and talks to Jamie about the situation. Then Dad suggests that they go over to the main offender's house to try and talk out their problem. Of course there are two sides to the story, but talking brings them both out enough to accomplish a true reconciliation.

Here are some points you may note from this story.

- Going *to* another family to work something out between kids is unusual in this day of isolation. But it can have surprising success, if it doesn't begin with a threat. Too often we forget the Matthew 18 advice of first going directly to the other person in trying to resolve a problem.
- Establish your child's confidence in your loyalty before you take him or her to face someone else. If your child refuses to take a proper share of responsibility for the problem, don't abandon the child by pressuring him or her in front of the other family. Instead, suggest that you may need a little more time to think about the whole thing, and you'll get back in touch to conclude the conversation later.
- In Jamie's story, as in most, there are two sides. The "villain's" feelings must be dealt with, too, before genuine peace and reconciliation are established. Otherwise, pressure from the other boy's father might have ended the street attacks, but Jamie would have had an enemy for years to come. And enemies always find ways to make life miserable.

In this story, the father not only models the way of dealing with anger by talking it out, but he walks his son through the steps to accomplish a resolution.

Snowman Down

Jamie is proud of the huge snowman he has just built in the front yard. But when he goes into the house to get a scarf and hat for it, his little brother, Robbie, knocks the snowman down. Jamie is furious and runs out screaming at his brother, actually wanting to hurt him with the snowballs he hurls.

Finally the boys' mother takes them inside and helps them talk out their angry feelings.

Mother's success in settling the fight is based on her practice of some important principles:

- She's not there to mete out judgment, but to help each child be understood by the other. Her goal is to help them talk it out.
- In kneeling with an arm around each of them, she a) separates them from each other while still keeping them close to her, b) gives them a sense of security, and c) maintains enough body contact with the boys to sense the subsiding of

5

their tension.

- Mother first asks Robbie to share his side, while assuring Jamie that his turn will come soon. At this point she does not pass judgment or express sympathy, but lets the story be told.

- Though Jamie was the "victim," he hears something of his brother's side and has time to cool down a little. His telling provides a further release, especially when he sees that Robbie is hearing and being touched by what he says.

- Robbie is given a chance at restitution without it being a punishment. In fact, he gets to play in the snow, too.

Late Again

When Jamie saw his mom standing at the window, he knew he was in trouble.

Until then he had completely forgotten her warning from the day before: "The next time you're late from school, Jamie, you'll be sorry."

And today he was late, but it wasn't his fault. Just before school was out, his teacher had asked him to take the big envelope with lunch money in it to the office and give it to Miss Crumble, the secretary.

"Don't give it to anyone else," she had said. "It is very important that you give it only to her."

Jamie felt proud that his teacher had asked him to take the money. But when he got to the office, Miss Crumble wasn't there. He waited and waited. The bell rang to dismiss school for the day, and still Miss Crumble didn't come. Jamie could hear all the kids laughing and talking out in the hall. In a few

minutes it got quieter as they all left the building.

Finally he heard the clicking heels of someone walking down the hall. He looked out the door and was glad to see Miss Crumble. He handed her the envelope and ran back to his classroom for his coat.

And that was why he was late. He hadn't thought about getting in trouble till now, when he saw Mom standing with her hands on her hips.

He opened the door, but before he could say a word, she called from the living room. "James Edward, come in here right now!" When she called him James Edward, he knew he was in trouble for sure. "You are more than ten minutes late getting home from school. Do you remember what I said?"

"But, Mom—" Jamie started.

"If anything should happen to you, I need to know about it. If you're late all the time, I don't know when you might really need help. Now, because you were late again, I'm afraid you can't play with David this afternoon as you had planned."

"That's not fair!" Jamie exploded. He was so angry that he didn't even think about trying to explain *why* he was late. "You're mean! You don't even know what happened!"

"James," Mom said quietly, "go into your room till you can speak in a more respectful way."

Jamie stomped down the hall. Mom watched while he went into his room and slammed the door.

It isn't fair. She didn't even ask why I was late. Jamie flopped down on his bed. *And it wasn't even my fault. I was trying to do something* good.

The more he thought about it, the angrier he got. Jamie started to cry. *Just because I'm a kid and she's a grown-up, she wins,* he thought.

In a while he was all worn out from crying. He sat up on the edge of his bed. *Pretty soon the whole day is going to be wasted,* Jamie thought. *Maybe I should go tell Mom what really happened.*

But as soon as he thought of that idea, he started to feel mad again. "She didn't care enough to ask the first time," he said out loud, even though there was no one there to hear. "She probably doesn't want to know. Maybe I'll never talk to her again. That would show her."

But Jamie knew that would never work. Talking was the only way out, and he hadn't tried it yet—at least not in a respectful way.

He opened the door and walked slowly down the hall. Mom was at her desk in the dining room, writing a letter. Jamie stood where she couldn't see him for a minute, getting up his courage.

"Mom," he finally said in a small voice, "I was really mad that you didn't ask me *why* I was late before you said I couldn't play with David. May I tell you now?"

"Sure, Jamie."

Jamie told about taking the envelope to the office and having to wait for Miss Crumble. "After that I came straight home," he finished.

"Oh, Jamie," Mom said, holding her arms out wide. "That's a very good reason for being late. I'm sorry for not asking you in the beginning. I guess I was too worried about you to think that I should have asked. Can you forgive me?"

Jamie hugged his mom hard. "Yes, I can forgive you. I'm sorry you were worried."

"I'm glad we got it worked out," Mom said.

"Me, too," Jamie answered. He did feel better. "Can I go play with David now?"

"Sure," Mom said. "Have fun." ■

From God's Word

A gentle answer turns away
   wrath,
   but a harsh word stirs up
   anger.
The tongue of the wise
   commends knowledge,
   but the mouth of the fool
   gushes folly.
   from Proverbs 15:1, 2 (NIV)

13

Think It Through

Ask your children these questions and discuss the answers.

1. How did the fact that Jamie had been late several times before affect this situation?
   If this had been only the first time he had been late, it probably wouldn't have mattered. But he had been late often, so his mom was trying to get him to obey and had promised a consequence.

2. Why didn't Jamie's mom learn about why he was late when he first came in the door?

3. What do you think would have happened if Jamie had been able to tell his mom right away, in a respectful way, what had happened to him?

4. How did going to his room help Jamie?
   It allowed him space to get control of his anger and come back to talk to his mom in a good way.

5. When Jamie was angry, he yelled, stomped his feet, and slammed the door. How do *you* show it when you're angry? Next time, try talking about it instead!

6. Have you ever felt you were punished unfairly? What did you do about it?

Windy Britches

Jamie didn't like the way Antonio bragged about everything. He bragged when he kicked the ball hardest. He bragged when he wore a new jacket to school.

"Hey, look at me," Antonio yelled one day during recess. "I bet you can't climb up here."

Jamie looked. Antonio had climbed up one pole of the swing set to the top. Jamie went to another pole. He jumped and tried to pull himself up, but he couldn't get more than a foot or two off the ground before he'd slide back down.

"What's the matter, Jamie?" Antonio called. "You too weak to climb up here?"

Just then Jamie noticed a hole torn right in the seat of Antonio's pants.

"No," Jamie retorted, "I'm not too weak. I just don't have windy britches to show off."

"What do you mean, 'windy britches'?"

"Britches are pants, and yours have got a hole," Jamie yelled. "Look, everybody. Antonio's got a hole in his pants that the wind blows through."

Everyone laughed and pointed. "Windy britches, windy britches," they chanted.

Antonio's face was red as he slid back down.

Just then the bell rang. Jamie turned and ran with everyone toward the door. But before he got there, Antonio crashed into him from the side.

"Come on now, boys," said their teacher, "let's

go inside like gentlemen."

But as they squeezed through the door, Antonio said to Jamie, "You just wait. You'll be sorry."

Jamie didn't care. For once, Antonio wasn't such a big shot.

But when Jamie started home that afternoon, Antonio was waiting with two other boys. Jamie crossed the street. The boys crossed over, too.

"Scared?" Antonio said, as Jamie walked toward them. Then he ran up to Jamie and knocked him over. Every time Jamie tried to get up, one of the boys tripped or pushed him. They didn't quit until Jamie was so mad that he cried.

The next day it happened again. Jamie tried to go home a different direction, but Antonio and his friends saw him and caught him.

The third day it happened again. That night Jamie's dad sat down with him after dinner.

"Mom says that for three days you've been coming home from school all dirty. Have you been having some trouble?" Dad asked.

"I guess," Jamie said. "Some guys keep jumping me on my way home."

"What guys? Do you know them?"

"One of them is in my class."

"What's his name?" Dad asked.

"Antonio. I'd like to beat him up."

"Do you think that would help?"

"Well, I can't because there are three of them," Jamie replied. "But I'd still like to."

"I guess you would. It makes me angry, too, just to hear about it. How did all this start?"

Jamie told his father about Antonio's bragging

and teasing and about the "windy britches."

Jamie's dad listened quietly. Then he said, "You're pretty angry about all this, aren't you?"

"Yeah," said Jamie.

"You remember what we say about being angry, but not too angry to talk? Do you think you could talk to Antonio about it?"

"I don't know," said Jamie. "I guess so."

"Okay, then," Dad said. "You wait here. I've got a phone call to make."

Soon he came back. "I know Antonio's dad," he said. "I called to see if Antonio would be willing to talk, too. But first let's pray about it, okay?"

Jamie nodded, and Dad asked God to help the boys tell each other how angry they were, listen to

each other's feelings, and work out their problems.

When they got to Antonio's house, Jamie was scared. He kept his eyes on the floor so he wouldn't have to look at Antonio.

At first the boys didn't want to talk. But their dads helped them tell the story as they each saw it.

Jamie's dad said, "Jamie, how do you think Antonio felt with everyone laughing at him?"

"Not very good," answered Jamie. "But he made fun of me when I couldn't climb the swing."

The boys could see that the things they had said had embarrassed and angered each other.

"I'm sorry for making fun of you for not climbing the pole," Antonio finally said.

"And I'm sorry for calling you 'windy britches,'" said Jamie.

"That's all right," Antonio answered. "And I won't jump on you anymore after school."

The boys shook hands. Then they went outside to play while their dads talked about baseball. ■

20

From God's Word

If your brother sins against you,
go and show him his fault,
just between the two of you.
If he listens to you,
you have won your brother
over.
—*from Matthew 18:15 (NIV)*

21

Think It Through

Ask your children these questions and discuss the answers.

1. Why did Jamie call Antonio "Windy Britches"?

2. Why do you think Jamie didn't tell his mom or dad about Antonio jumping on him the first day it happened?
Maybe he didn't want to be a tattletale. Maybe he knew that Antonio had reason to be mad at him.

3. Jamie told his dad that he wished he could beat Antonio up. What do you think might have happened if he had tried?
Even if he succeeded, he might have made a long-term enemy. He certainly would not have won a friend, as he did by talking things out.

4. Is there anyone you are very angry at for something he or she did to you? How might talking to that person improve things?

Snowman Down

Jamie's hands were wet and cold, but he couldn't quit yet—not until he had finished his huge snowman. It was taller than he was, and he still hadn't put the head on.

Jamie rolled a snowball the size of a basketball and carried it over to the snowman. He lifted it as high as he could, but he couldn't reach the top.

Then Jamie remembered the big, white plastic bucket that Dad used when he washed the car. He found the bucket in the garage and dragged it out. Standing on top of it, he was just tall enough to put the head on. What a great snowman! Jamie ran into the house to get the finishing touches.

"Hey, Mom! I need an old hat, a scarf, and a carrot," he yelled, stamping snow off his boots.

"What for?" she called from the back room.

"For my snowman," Jamie said. "But don't

come see now. I want to finish him first."

Jamie's little brother, Robbie, raced into the living room to look out the window.

"Mom," Jamie called again, "I need some coal, too, for his mouth and eyes and buttons. You know—like Frosty."

"You might find some barbecue charcoal from last summer on the back porch. That ought to do."

It didn't take Jamie long to round up the things he needed and head back outside. But when he opened the front door and looked out, he stopped short. The giant snowman had tumbled down. The head and the big middle ball lay on the ground, smashed into pieces.

Then from behind the great, round, bottom ball, Robbie appeared. He looked at Jamie with wide eyes. "I wanted to help," he whimpered.

"You ruined my snowman! You knocked him down!" Jamie screamed, throwing down the things he held. "I worked all morning on that snowman!"

"I just wanted to climb up and touch him," Robbie said, backing away from the big piles of broken snow. "I didn't mean to knock him down."

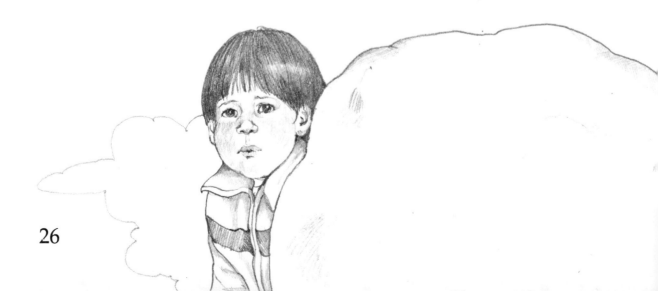

Jamie was so mad that he picked up a snowball and threw it at Robbie as hard as he could. It wasn't like a snowball fight for fun—Jamie wanted to hurt Robbie. He took another snowball and hit Robbie hard, right in the face.

Robbie began to cry, but Jamie didn't stop. He threw more and more snowballs until Mom suddenly appeared at the door.

"Jamie, stop it! What's going on out here?"

"He knocked down my snowman on purpose," Jamie yelled. He was so mad that he was almost crying, too.

"No, I didn't," cried Robbie. "I didn't mean to. But he hit me in the face on purpose."

Mom took one boy with each hand and led them both into the house. Then she knelt down between them, one arm tightly around each. She hugged them until Robbie's crying slowed to big sobs.

"Now, Robbie, why don't you tell me what happened first, and then Jamie can have his turn."

Robbie told how he had watched Jamie work on the snowman and wanted to help. When he got his snow clothes on, he just couldn't wait for Jamie. He climbed up on the bucket, just to touch the snowman, and then it fell over. "I didn't mean to knock him down," Robbie finished.

"Jamie, now you tell Robbie how you are feeling," Mom said.

Jamie told about how hard he had worked and what a good snowman he had built. "It really made me mad when I saw him knocked down," he said. Jamie wasn't yelling anymore. He was still angry, but he wasn't too angry to talk. But suddenly Robbie started to cry again.

"Why are you crying now, Robbie?" asked Mom.

"'Cause I'm sad," he sniffed. "I didn't mean to knock the snowman down. I'm sorry, Jamie."

Jamie knew that Robbie hadn't done it on purpose, but it was still hard to forgive him. "You

might be sorry, but the snowman's still in pieces,''
he pouted.

"Well," Mom said, "do you think Robbie could
help you build it back up again?''

"I don't know. He's too little," answered Jamie.

"No, I'm not," said Robbie. "I'll do just what
you tell me."

"Well, okay. Let's go," Jamie said, taking
Robbie's arm. "Hey," he added, as they went out
the door, "I'm sorry for hitting you in the face with
that snowball, too." ■

From God's Word

In your anger do not sin:
Do not let the sun go down
while you are still angry,
and do not give the devil
a foothold. . .
Do not let any unwholesome talk
come out of your mouths,
but only what is helpful
for building others up.
—*from Ephesians 4:26, 27, 29 (NIV)*

30

Think It Through

1. What made the snowman so important to Jamie?

2. What was Robbie trying to do?

3. Why did Robbie start crying the second time—in the house?

4. Why did Jamie forgive Robbie?

5. What do you think happened when the boys went back outside?

Books for you,
containing stories
to read aloud and discuss
with your children

STORYBOOKS FOR *Caring* PARENTS

Scared, But Not Too Scared *(to think)*
Bored, But Not Too Bored *(to pretend)*
Angry, But Not Too Angry *(to talk)*
Tired, But Not Too Tired *(to finish)*